DRINK
ME NOW

DRINK ME NOW

150 COCKTAILS FOR ANY EMERGENCY

hamlyn

An Hachette UK Company
www.hachette.co.uk

First published in Great Britain in 2016 by Hamlyn,
a division of Octopus Publishing Group Ltd
Carmelite House
50 Victoria Embankment
London EC4Y 0DZ
www.octopusbooks.co.uk
www.octopusbooksusa.com

This material was previously published in
200 Cocktails, 200 Classic Cocktails, Poptails
and The Skinny Sipper's Low-calorie Cocktail Bible.

Copyright © Octopus Publishing Group Ltd 2016

Distributed in the US by Hachette Book Group
1290 Avenue of the Americas
4th and 5th Floors
New York, NY 10020

Distributed in Canada by Canadian Manda Group
664 Annette St.
Toronto, Ontario, Canada M6S 2C8

ISBN 978-0-600-63366-2

A CIP catalogue record for this book is available
from the British Library

Printed and bound in China
10 9 8 7 6 5 4 3 2 1

The measure that has been used in the recipes
is based on a bar jigger, which is 25 ml (1 fl oz).
If preferred, a different volume can be used,
providing the proportions are kept constant
within a drink and suitable adjustments are made
to spoon measurements, where they occur.

Standard level spoon measurements are used
in all recipes.
1 tablespoon = one 15 ml spoon
1 teaspoon = one 5 ml spoon

The Department of Health advises that eggs should
not be consumed raw. This book contains some recipes
made with raw eggs. It is prudent for vulnerable people
such as pregnant and nursing mothers, invalids and the
elderly to avoid these recipes.

This book includes recipes made with nuts and nut
derivatives. It is advisable for those with known
allergic reactions to nuts and nut derivatives to avoid
these recipes. It is also prudent to check the label of
pre-prepared ingredients for the possible inclusion
of nut derivatives.

The UK Health Department recommends that men
do not regularly exceed 3–4 units of alcohol a day
and women 2–3 units a day, a unit being defined
as 10 ml of pure alcohol, the equivalent of a single
measure (25 ml) of spirits. The US Department of
Health and Human Services recommends that men
do not regularly exceed 2 drinks a day and women
1 drink a day, a drink being defined as 0.5 oz of pure
alcohol, the equivalent of 1.5 oz of 80-proof distilled
spirits. Those who regularly drink more than this run
an increasingly significant risk of illness and death
from a number of conditions. In addition, women
who are pregnant or trying to conceive should
avoid drinking alcohol.

CONTENTS

INTRODUCTION

INGREDIENTS

Good cocktails, like good food, are based around quality ingredients. Using fresh and homemade ingredients, as with cooking, can often make a huge difference between a good drink and an outstanding drink.

ICE This is a key part of cocktails and you'll need lots of it. Purchase it from your supermarket or freeze big tubs of water, then crack this up to use in your drinks. If you're hosting a party, it may be worthwhile finding out if you have a local ice supplier, as this can be much more cost effective.

CITRUS JUICE It's important to use fresh citrus juice in your drinks; bottled versions taste awful and will not produce good drinks. Store your fruit out of the refrigerator at room temperature. Look for a soft-skinned fruit for juicing, which you can do with a juicer or citrus press. You can keep fresh citrus juice for a couple of days in the refrigerator, sealed to prevent oxidation.

SUGAR SYRUP You can buy sugar syrup to use when making cocktails or you can make your own. The key when preparing sugar syrups is to use a 1:1 ratio of sugar to liquid. You can use different types of sugar to make sugar syrup. White sugar acts as a flavour enhancer, while dark sugars have their own unique, toffee-like flavours, which work well with dark spirits.

MAKES 1 litre (1¾ pints)

BASIC SUGAR SYRUP

1 litre (1¾ pints) hot water
1 kg (2 lb) caster sugar

Combine the caster sugar with the hot water and stir until the sugar has dissolved. Allow to cool.

Decant the sugar syrup into a sterilized bottle and store in the refrigerator for up to 2 weeks.

FLAVOURED SYRUPS

Again, you can buy these or make your own. There are three options for creating your own flavoured syrups.

The first option is to add a shop-bought flavoured essence to a sugar syrup made on a 1:1 ratio as described on page 6. So, to make Rose Syrup, for example, add 25 ml (1 fl oz) rose essence to 1 kg (2 lb) caster sugar dissolved in 1 litre (1¾ pints) of hot water.

The second option for creating a flavoured syrup is to use equal measures of strong fruit-flavoured tea and caster sugar. So, to create 1 litre (1¾ pints) of Lemon & Ginger Syrup, for example, mix 1 litre (1¾ pints) hot lemon and ginger tea with 1 kg (2 lb) caster sugar and stir until dissolved. Ensure that you remember to remove the tea bags prior to adding the sugar or things are likely to get very sticky!

The final option is to create syrups from fresh fruit, herbs or spices.

MAKES 1 litre (1¾ pints)

BASIC FLAVOURED SYRUP

**250 g (8 oz) fruit or 3 tablespoons
of whole spices (not powdered)
1 litre (1¾ pints) water
1 kg (2 lb) caster sugar**

Remove any thick inedible peel from the fruit and remove any stalks, stones or pips as these will create a tannic flavour in your syrup.

Put the fruit or spices into a saucepan, add the water and bring to the boil. Reduce the heat and simmer for 30 minutes, topping up with water if required, or until the fruit is stripped of its colour. Taste the water to check how much of the flavour has leached into it.

Remove from the heat and strain into a heatproof bowl, discarding the fruit or spices. Mix the hot fruit or spice liquid with the sugar, stirring until dissolved. Allow to cool.

Decant the sugar syrup into a sterilized bottle and store in the refrigerator for up to 2 weeks.

CHOOSING A GLASS

There are thousands of different cocktails, but they all fall into one of three categories: long, short or shot. Long drinks generally have more mixer than alcohol and are often served with ice and a straw. The terms 'straight up' and 'on the rocks' are synonymous with the short drink, which tends to be more about the spirit, which is often combined with a single mixer, at most. Finally, there is the shot. These miniature cocktails are made up mainly from spirits and liqueurs and are designed to give a quick hit of alcohol. Cocktail glasses are tailored to the type of drinks they will contain.

CHAMPAGNE FLUTE

Used for Champagne or Champagne cocktails, the narrow mouth of the flute helps the drink to stay fizzy.

CHAMPAGNE SAUCER

These old-fashioned glasses are not very practical for serving Champagne because the drink quickly loses its fizz.

COUPETTE OR MARGARITA GLASS

When this type of glass is used for a Margarita (see page 294), the rim is dipped in salt. These glasses are used for Daiquiris and other fruit-based cocktails.

MARTINI GLASS

A martini glass, also known as a cocktail glass, is designed so that your hand can't warm the glass, making sure that the cocktail is served completely chilled.

HIGHBALL GLASS

A highball glass is suitable for any long cocktail, from the Cuba Libre (see page 304) to Long Island Iced Tea (see page 292).

COLLINS GLASS

This is similar to a highball glass but is slightly narrower.

WINE GLASS

Sangria (see page 210) is often served in a wine glass, but these glasses are not usually used for cocktails.

OLD-FASHIONED GLASS

Also known as a rocks glass, the old-fashioned glass is great for any drink that's served on the rocks or straight up. It's also good for muddled drinks (see page 13).

SHOT GLASS

Shot glasses are often found in two sizes – for a single or double measure. They are ideal for a single mouthful, which can range from a Tequila Slammer (see page 222) to the more decadent layered B-52 (see page 146).

HURRICANE GLASS

This type of glass is mostly found in beach bars, where it is used to serve creamy rum-based drinks.

TODDY GLASS

A toddy glass is generally used for a hot drink, such as an Early Night (see page 134).

SLING GLASS

This has a very short-stemmed base and is most famously used for a Singapore Sling (see page 310).

POPTAILS

Some recipes in this book are alcohol-infused popsicles, ices and slushes. These recipes are all based on popsicle moulds of about 100 ml (3½ fl oz). If you can't find any exactly this size, don't fret as you can use larger moulds and simply not fill them completely or use smaller moulds and make more. Always remember though that on filling the moulds, you want to leave a little space to allow for the poptails to expand a bit during freezing. To remove the poptails from their moulds, simply run a little hot water on the outside of the containers and pull out with the sticks.

Get creative! Nothing is set in stone – you can use virtually any freezable hygienic container you can get your hands on to make a poptail. Why not try plastic cups? Or make the Pomegranate, Vanilla and Vodka Ice Cubes (see page 246) and drop a few cubes into a glass of sparkling water to make a small aperitif. For a granita, follow the recipe instructions, but rather than filling popsicle moulds, pour into a suitable-sized freezer-safe container, cover and freeze, stirring with a fork every couple of hours to break up the granita a bit. Another option is to make slushes, sort of like a frozen Margarita. Freeze these in a freezer-safe container for about 4 hours, stirring every hour to help freeze evenly, then pour into ice-cold glasses and serve.

USEFUL EQUIPMENT

There are a few tools that are worth investing in if you are planning to make cocktails.

BOTTLE OPENER

Choose a bottle opener with two attachments, one for metal-topped bottles and a corkscrew for wine bottles.

POURERS

A pourer is inserted into the top of a spirit bottle to enable the spirit to flow in a controlled manner.

MEASURE OR JIGGER

Single and double measures are available and are essential when you are mixing ingredients so that the proportions are always the same. One measure is 25 ml (1 fl oz).

MUDDLER

Similar to a pestle, which will work just as well, a muddler, or muddling stick, is used to crush fruit or herbs in a glass or shaker for drinks like the Mojito (see page 290).

COCKTAIL SHAKER

The Boston shaker is the simplest option, but it needs to be used in conjunction with a hawthorne strainer. Alternatively you could choose a shaker with a built-in strainer.

HAWTHORNE STRAINER

This type of strainer is often used in conjunction with a Boston shaker, but a simple tea strainer will also work well.

MIXING GLASS

A mixing glass is used for those drinks that require only a gentle stirring before they are poured or strained.

BAR SPOON

Similar to a teaspoon but with a long handle, a bar spoon is used for stirring, layering and muddling drinks.

FOOD PROCESSOR

A food processor or blender is useful for making frozen cocktails and smoothies.

MIXOLOGY MASTERCLASS

With just a few basic techniques, your bartending skills will be complete. Follow the step-by-step instructions to hone your craft and mix perfect cocktails.

SHAKING

This is the best-known cocktail technique and probably the one that you will use most often, so it's important to get right. Shaking is used to mix ingredients quickly and thoroughly, and to chill the drink before serving.

1. Half-fill a cocktail shaker with ice cubes or cracked or crushed ice.
2. If the recipe calls for a chilled glass, add a few ice cubes and some cold water to the glass, swirl it around and discard.
3. Add the recipe ingredients to the shaker and shake until a frost forms on the outside of the shaker. Use both hands, one at each end, so that it doesn't slip.
4. Strain the cocktail into the glass and serve.

BLENDING

Frozen cocktails and smoothies are blended with ice in a blender until they are of a smooth consistency. A frozen Daiquiri or Margarita is made using a virtually identical recipe to the unfrozen versions but with a scoop of crushed ice added to the blender before blending on high speed. Be careful not to add too much ice to the recipe as this will dilute the cocktail. It's best to add a little at a time.

BUILDING

This is a straightforward technique that involves nothing more than putting the ingredients together in the correct order.

1. Have all the ingredients for the cocktail to hand. Chill the glass, if required.
2. Add each ingredient in recipe order, making sure that all measures are exact.

DOUBLE-STRAINING

When you want to prevent all traces of puréed fruit and ice fragments from entering the glass, use a shaker with a built-in strainer in conjunction with a hawthorne strainer. Alternatively, strain through a fine strainer.

MUDDLING

Muddling is a technique that is used to bring out the flavours of herbs and fruit using a blunt tool called a muddler, and the best-known muddled drink is the Mojito (see page 290).

1. Add mint leaves to a highball glass, then add some sugar syrup and some lime wedges.
2. Hold the glass firmly and use a muddler or pestle to press down. Twist and press to release the flavours.
3. Continue this for about 30 seconds, then top up the glass with crushed ice and add the remaining ingredients.

LAYERING

A number of spirits can be served layered on top of each other, and because some spirits are lighter than others, they will float on top of your cocktail. One of the best-known layered drinks is the Grasshopper (see page 176).

1. Pour the first ingredient into a glass, taking care that it does not touch the sides.
2. Position a bar spoon in the centre of the glass, rounded part down and facing you. Rest the spoon against the side of the glass as you pour the second ingredient down the spoon. It should float on top of the first liquid, creating a separate layer.
3. Repeat with the third ingredient, then carefully remove the spoon.

ALL ABOUT ME

TIJUANA SLING

3½ measures tequila
1½ measures crème de cassis
1½ measures lime juice
4 dashes Peychaud's bitters
ice cubes
7 measures ginger ale

TO DECORATE
lime slices
blueberries

Pour the tequila, crème de cassis, lime juice and bitters into a cocktail shaker. Add 8–10 ice cubes and shake vigorously.

Pour into 2 highball glasses and top up with the ginger ale. Decorate each glass with lime slices and blueberries and serve.

LUSH CRUSH

4 strawberries, plus extra to decorate

2 dashes sugar syrup

4 lime wedges

2 measures Absolut Kurant vodka

ice cubes

chilled Champagne, to top up

Muddle the strawberries, sugar syrup and lime wedges in the bottom of a cocktail shaker. Add the vodka and some ice cubes.

Shake and double-strain into 2 chilled Champagne flutes, then top up with Champagne. Decorate each glass with a sliced strawberry and serve.

VANILLA VODKA SOUR

ice cubes
4 measures vanilla vodka
1 measure sugar syrup
2 egg whites
3 measures lemon juice
10 dashes Angostura bitters, to decorate

Put 8–10 ice cubes into a cocktail shaker. Add the vodka, sugar syrup, egg whites and lemon juice and shake until a frost forms on the outside of the shaker.

Pour into 2 martini glasses. Shake the bitters on top to decorate and serve.

GINGERSNAP

ice cubes
6 measures vodka
2 measures ginger wine
soda water, to top up

Put 4–6 ice cubes into 2 old-fashioned glasses. Pour the
vodka and ginger wine over the ice and stir lightly. Top up
with soda water and serve.

AMERICAN BELLE

1 measure cherry liqueur
1 measure Amaretto di Saronno
1 measure bourbon

Pour the cherry liqueur, Amaretto and bourbon into
2 shot glasses. Stir lightly to mix and serve.

BERLIN BLONDE

2 measures dark rum

2 measures Cointreau

2 measures double cream

ice cubes

TO DECORATE

ground cinnamon

maraschino cherries

Pour the rum, Cointreau and cream into a cocktail shaker, add 8–10 ice cubes and shake.

Double-strain into 2 chilled martini glasses. Decorate each glass with a sprinkling of ground cinnamon and some cherries on cocktail sticks and serve.

SILK STOCKING

drinking chocolate powder
1½ measures tequila
1½ measures white crème de cacao
7 measures single cream
4 teaspoons grenadine
ice cubes

Dampen the rim of 2 chilled martini glasses and dip them into a saucer of drinking chocolate powder.

Pour the tequila, crème de cacao, cream and grenadine into a cocktail shaker and add 8–10 ice cubes. Shake vigorously for 10 seconds, then strain into the prepared glasses and serve.

X-RATED MILKSHAKE

2 measures Frangelico hazelnut liqueur
2 measures Bailey's Irish Cream
2 measures single cream
2 measures dark crème de cacao
1 measure clear honey
8 strawberries
1 small banana
crushed ice
2 measures chocolate sauce, to decorate

Put the Frangelico, Bailey's, cream, crème de cacao, honey, strawberries and banana into a food processor or blender with some crushed ice and blend until slushy.

Decorate the insides of 2 large hurricane glasses with chocolate sauce. Pour in the drink and serve.

ALL ABOUT ME

BERRY COLLINS

8 raspberries, plus extra to decorate
8 blueberries
1–2 dashes strawberry syrup
crushed ice
4 measures gin
4 teaspoons lemon juice
sugar syrup, to taste
soda water, to top up

Put the berries and strawberry syrup into 2 highball glasses
and muddle together.

Fill each glass with crushed ice. Add the gin, lemon juice and
sugar syrup, stir, then top up with the soda water. Decorate
each glass with raspberries and serve.

ZAN LA CAY

5 cm (2 inch) piece cucumber

1 green cardamom pod

3 teaspoons crème de peche

2 teaspoons sugar syrup

ice cubes

4 measures chilled Champagne

cucumber slice, to decorate

Muddle the cucumber and cardamom pod in the bottom of a cocktail shaker, then add the crème de peche and sugar syrup.

Add a couple of ice cubes, pour in the Champagne and stir before straining into a Champagne flute. Decorate with a cucumber slice and serve.

COBBLER FIZZ

3 slices mandarin
2 raspberries, plus extra to decorate
2 teaspoons sugar syrup
1 measure fino sherry
4 measures chilled prosecco

Add the mandarin, raspberries and sugar syrup to a
cocktail shaker and muddle. Add the sherry and shake.

Strain into a Champagne flute and top up with the
prosecco. Decorate with a raspberry on a cocktail
stick and serve.

SOUTHSIDE

ice cubes

2 measures gin

4 teaspoons lime juice

4 teaspoons sugar syrup

5 mint leaves, plus extra to decorate

Add all the ingredients to a cocktail shaker. Shake and
strain into a martini glass. Decorate with a mint leaf
and serve.

BITTER SPRING

ice cubes
1 measure Aperol
2 measures grapefruit juice
4 measures soda water
grapefruit wedge, to decorate

Pour the Aperol, grapefruit juice and soda water into an
old-fashioned glass full of ice cubes and stir. Decorate
with a grapefruit wedge and serve.

MOON RIVER

ice cubes
1 measure dry gin
1 measure apricot brandy
1 measure Cointreau
½ measure Galliano
½ measure lemon juice
maraschino cherries, to decorate

Put some ice cubes into a cocktail shaker. Pour the gin, apricot brandy, Cointreau, Galliano and lemon juice over the ice.

Shake, then strain into 2 chilled martini glasses. Drop a cherry into each glass and serve.

BELLINITINI

I½ measures vodka
½ measure peach schnapps
2 teaspoons peach juice
2 measures Champagne
peach slice, to decorate

Pour the vodka, schnapps and peach juice into
a cocktail shaker and shake well.

Pour into a chilled martini glass and top up with
Champagne. Decorate with a peach slice and serve.

WATERMELON & BASIL SMASH

ice cubes

2 measures gin

3 x I cm (½ inch) cubes watermelon

3 basil leaves, plus extra to decorate

2 teaspoons sugar syrup

Add all the ingredients to a cocktail shaker and shake well.

Strain into a chilled martini glass. Decorate with a basil leaf floated on the surface of the liquid and serve.

BEETNICK

1½ measures vodka
I measure beetroot juice
I measure orange juice
2 teaspoons lemon juice
I teaspoon agave syrup
ice cubes
orange twist, to decorate

Combine the vodka, beetroot, orange and lemon juices
and agave syrup in a cocktail shaker with some ice cubes.

Shake well, until a frost forms on the outside of the shaker,
then strain into a martini glass. Decorate with an orange
twist and serve.

GINGER RICKY

4 x 2.5 cm (I inch) cubes pineapple
2 lime wedges
1½ measures London dry gin
½ measure ginger juice (see tip)
I teaspoon lime juice
ice cubes
3½ measures ginger ale
pineapple wedge, to decorate

Muddle the pineapple and lime wedges in the bottom of a cocktail
shaker. Add the gin and ginger and lime juices and shake well.

Strain into a highball glass filled with ice cubes and top up with the
ginger ale. Decorate with a pineapple wedge and serve.

TIP

TO MAKE GINGER JUICE, PEEL A LARGE PIECE OF FRESH ROOT
GINGER AND BLITZ IN A BLENDER OR FOOD PROCESSOR. STRAIN
THE JUICE BEFORE USE.

PINK RUM

3 drops Angostura bitters

3–4 ice cubes

2 measures white rum

2 measures cranberry juice

1 measure soda water

lime slice, to decorate

Shake the bitters into a highball glass and swirl it around.

Add the ice cubes, then pour in the rum, cranberry juice and soda water. Decorate with a lime slice on a cocktail stick and serve.

JALISCO

crushed ice
1½ measures tequila
10 cm (4 inch) piece cucumber
1 coriander sprig
2 teaspoons lime juice
4 pineapple wedges
1 teaspoon agave syrup
ice cubes

TO DECORATE
twist of black pepper
cucumber slice

Add all ingredients to a food processor or blender with some ice cubes and blend until well combined.

Pour into a Collins glass, top with black pepper and a cucumber slice and serve.

LONG DAY AT
THE OFFICE

STORM AT SEA

4 measures cranberry juice

2 measures pineapple juice

4 teaspoons elderflower cordial

16–20 ice cubes

3 measures Blavod vodka

Pour the cranberry and pineapple juices and the elderflower cordial into a cocktail shaker with half the ice cubes and shake to mix.

Strain into 2 old-fashioned glasses over the remaining ice cubes. Add the vodka slowly, which will separate briefly, and serve immediately.

OFFSHORE

2 measures white rum
2 measures tequila gold
12 mint leaves, plus extra to decorate
4 pineapple chunks
6 measures pineapple juice
2 measures single cream
crushed ice

Put the rum, tequila, mint leaves, pineapple chunks, pineapple juice and single cream into a food processor or blender with some crushed ice and blend until the mixture is slushy.

Transfer to 2 hurricane glasses, decorate each with mint leaves and serve.

RUSSIAN SPRING PUNCH

ice cubes
1 measure crème de cassis
2 measures lemon juice
4 tablespoons sugar syrup
chilled Champagne, to top up
4 measures Absolut vodka

TO DECORATE
lemon slices
mixed berries

Fill 2 highball glasses with ice cubes. Pour the crème de
cassis, lemon juice and sugar syrup over the ice.

Add the Champagne and vodka at the same time
(this prevents excessive fizzing) and stir. Decorate each
glass with a lemon slice and some berries and serve.

$$E = MC^2$$

crushed ice
4 measures Southern Comfort
2 measures lemon juice
1 measure maple syrup
chilled Champagne, to top up
lemon rind strips, to decorate

Put some crushed ice into a cocktail shaker. Pour the
Southern Comfort, lemon juice and maple syrup over
the ice and shake until a frost forms on the outside of
the shaker.

Strain into 2 Champagne flutes and top up with
Champagne. Decorate each glass with a lemon rind
strip and serve.

SAPPHIRE MARTINI

ice cubes

4 measures gin

1 measure blue Curaçao

red or blue cocktail cherries, to decorate

Put 8 ice cubes into a cocktail shaker. Pour the gin and blue Curaçao over the ice and shake well to mix.

Strain into 2 martini glasses. Carefully drop a cherry into each glass and serve.

GIN GARDEN MARTINI

½ cucumber, peeled and chopped, plus extra peeled slices to decorate

1 measure elderflower cordial

4 measures gin

2 measures pressed apple juice

ice cubes

Muddle the cucumber in the bottom of a cocktail shaker with the elderflower cordial. Add the gin, apple juice and some ice cubes.

Shake and double-strain into 2 chilled martini glasses. Decorate each glass with peeled cucumber slices and serve.

BRAIN HAEMORRHAGE

1 measure peach schnapps
1 measure Bailey's Irish Cream
6 dashes grenadine

Pour the schnapps into 2 chilled shot glasses. Using the back of a bar spoon, slowly float the Bailey's over the schnapps to form a separate layer.

Very gently, drop the grenadine on top of the Bailey's – it will gradually ease through this top layer and fall to the bottom of the glass – and serve.

FIFTH AVENUE

2 measures crème de cacao

2 measures apricot brandy

2 measures single cream

Pour the crème de cacao into 2 straight-sided shot glasses. Using the back of a bar spoon, slowly float the apricot brandy over the crème de cacao to form a separate layer.

Layer the cream over the apricot brandy in the same way and serve.

GIN CUCUMBER COOLER

2 measures gin

5 mint leaves, plus an extra sprig to decorate

5 slices cucumber

3 measures apple juice

3 measures soda water

ice cubes

Add the gin, mint and cucumber to a Collins glass and gently muddle. Leave to stand for a couple of minutes.

Add the apple juice, soda water and some ice cubes. Decorate with a sprig of mint and serve.

CAMOMILE COLLINS

2 measures gin
1 camomile tea bag
1 measure lemon juice
1 measure sugar syrup
4 measures soda water
ice cubes
lemon slice, to decorate

Pour the gin into a Collins glass and add the tea bag. Stir the tea bag and gin together until the gin is infused with camomile flavour, about 5 minutes.

Remove the tea bag and fill the glass with ice cubes. Add the remaining ingredients, decorate with a lemon slice and serve.

GINGER FIX

ice cubes
1 measure blended Scotch whisky
1 measure ginger wine
2 dashes Angostura bitters
4 measures soda water
lemon wedge, to decorate

Fill the Collins glass with ice cubes, add the remaining ingredients and stir. Decorate with a lemon wedge and serve.

JACK ROSE

ice cubes
2 measures apple brandy
3 teaspoons grenadine
4 teaspoons lemon juice

Add all the ingredients to a cocktail shaker. Shake, strain
into a martini glass and serve.

BLANC MONT BLANC

5 white grapes, plus extra to decorate

I measure vodka

I measure blanc vermouth

I measure lemon juice

I measure sugar syrup

ice cubes

Muddle the grapes in the bottom of a cocktail shaker.
Add the vodka, blanc vermouth, lemon juice and sugar
syrup, then fill the shaker with ice cubes.

Shake and strain into a martini glass. Decorate with
a grape on a cocktail stick and serve.

FRESH PALOMA

½ pink grapefruit, peeled
ice cubes
2 measures blanco tequila
2 measures soda water
1 teaspoon agave syrup
pink grapefruit wedge, to decorate

Juice the pink grapefruit and pour the juice into a Collins glass full of ice cubes.

Add the remaining ingredients, decorate with a grapefruit wedge and serve.

STONE FENCE

I crisp apple, plus an apple slice, to decorate
ice cubes
2 measures rye whiskey
I measure soda water

Juice the apple and pour the juice into an old-fashioned
glass full of ice cubes.

Add the whiskey and soda water. Decorate with an apple
slice and serve.

LAILA COCKTAIL

2 lime wedges

2 strawberries

4 blueberries, plus extra to decorate

1 dash mango purée

1 measure raspberry vodka

ice cubes

Muddle the lime wedges, berries, and mango purée in the bottom
of a cocktail shaker. Add the vodka and some ice cubes.

Shake vigorously and double-strain into a chilled martini glass.
Decorate with 3 extra blueberries on a cocktail stick.

HAIR RAISER

6–8 cracked ice cubes

2 measures vodka

2 measures sweet vermouth

2 measures tonic water

lemon and lime spirals, to decorate

Put 3–4 cracked ice cubes into 2 highball glasses. Pour the
vodka, vermouth and tonic water over the ice and stir lightly.
Decorate each glass with lemon and lime spirals and serve
with straws.

RUM OLD-FASHIONED

6 ice cubes
2 dashes Angostura bitters
2 dashes lime bitters
2 teaspoons caster sugar
1 measure water
4 measures white rum
1 measure dark rum
lime twists, to decorate

Put 2 ice cubes, both bitters, the sugar and water into 2 old-fashioned glasses and stir until the sugar has dissolved.

Add the white rum, stir and add the remaining ice cubes. Add the dark rum and stir again. Decorate each glass with a lime twist and serve.

A FRIEND IN NEED

MARGUERITE

ice cubes, plus cracked ice cubes to serve
6 measures vodka
juice of 2 lemons
juice of 1 orange
raspberry syrup, maraschino liqueur or grenadine, to taste

Put 8–10 ice cubes into a cocktail shaker. Pour the vodka, fruit juices and raspberry syrup, maraschino or grenadine over the ice and shake until a frost forms on the outside of the shaker.

Strain into 2 old-fashioned glasses filled with cracked ice cubes and serve.

MONTE CARLO SLING

10 grapes, plus extra to decorate

crushed ice

2 measures brandy

1 measure peach liqueur

2 measures ruby port

2 measures lemon juice

1 measure orange juice

2 dashes orange bitters

4 measures Champagne

Muddle 5 grapes in the bottom of each highball glass, then fill each glass with crushed ice.

Put all the other ingredients, except the Champagne, into a cocktail shaker and add more ice. Shake well.

Strain into the glasses and top up with the Champagne. Decorate each glass with grapes on cocktail sticks and serve.

TANQSTREAM

cracked ice cubes
4 measures Tanqueray gin
4 teaspoons lime juice
6 measures soda water or tonic water
4 teaspoons crème de cassis

TO DECORATE
lime slices
mixed berries

Put some cracked ice cubes with the gin and lime juice into a cocktail shaker and shake to mix.

Strain into 2 highball glasses, each half-filled with cracked ice cubes. For a dry Tanqstream, add soda water; for a less dry drink, add tonic water. Stir in the crème de cassis, decorate each glass with the lime slices and mixed berries and serve.

PINK CLOVER CLUB

ice cubes
juice of 2 limes
2 dashes grenadine
2 egg whites
6 measures gin
strawberry slices, to decorate

Put 8–10 ice cubes into a cocktail shaker. Pour the lime juice, grenadine, egg whites and gin over the ice and shake until a frost forms on the outside of the shaker.

Strain into 2 martini glasses. Decorate each glass with strawberry slices and serve.

BAJA SOUR

ice cubes
2½ measures tequila gold
4 teaspoons sugar syrup
2½ measures lemon juice
4 dashes orange bitters
I egg white
2 tablespoons amontillado sherry

TO DECORATE
lemon wedges
orange spirals

Put 8–10 ice cubes into a cocktail shaker with the tequila, sugar syrup, lemon juice, bitters and egg white and shake vigorously.

Pour into 2 highball glasses and drizzle over the sherry. Decorate each glass with a lemon wedge and an orange spiral and serve.

BATIDA MARACUJA

4 measures cachaça
4 passion fruit, cut in half and the pulp squeezed out
2 measures sugar syrup
2 measures lemon juice
ice cubes, plus crushed ice to serve

Put the cachaça, passion fruit pulp, sugar syrup and lemon
juice into a cocktail shaker and add some ice cubes.

Shake and strain into 2 highball glasses filled with crushed
ice and serve with straws.

MINT ZING TING

2 lime wedges

4 mint leaves

2 dashes sugar syrup

2 measures apple-flavoured vodka

ice cubes

cucumber strips, to decorate

Muddle the lime wedges, mint and sugar syrup in the
bottom of a cocktail shaker, then add the vodka and some
ice cubes. Shake briefly.

Strain into 2 chilled shot glasses, decorate each with
a cucumber strip and serve.

SPICED BERRY

ice cubes
2 measures Captain Morgan Spiced Rum
2 dashes lime juice
2 dashes raspberry purée
2 dashes sugar syrup
raspberries, to decorate

Put some ice cubes into a cocktail shaker, pour the rum,
lime juice, raspberry purée and sugar syrup over the ice
and shake briefly.

Strain into 2 chilled shot glasses, decorate each glass
with a raspberry and serve.

COWGIRL

2 measures chilled peach schnapps
1 measure Bailey's Irish Cream
peach wedges

Pour the schnapps into 2 shot glasses, then, using the back of a bar spoon, slowly float the Bailey's over the schnapps to form a separate layer.

Place a peach wedge on the rim of each glass – to be eaten after the shot has been drunk – and serve.

LYCHEE MARTINI

ice cubes
2 measures vodka
3 lychees, plus extra to decorate
I measure Triple Sec
3 teaspoons lemon juice

Add all the ingredients to a cocktail shaker and muddle.

Shake, then strain into a martini glass. Decorate with
a lychee on a cocktail stick and serve.

GIN CREAM SODA

ice cubes
2 measures gin
2 teaspoons lemon juice
4 measures cream soda

TO DECORATE
black cherry
lemon slice

Pour all the ingredients into a Collins glass full of ice cubes and
stir. Decorate with a cherry and a lemon slice and serve.

FRENCH 75

1 measure gin

3 teaspoons lemon juice

3 teaspoons sugar syrup

4 measures chilled Champagne

lemon twist, to decorate

Pour the gin, lemon juice and sugar syrup into a cocktail shaker and shake.

Strain into a Champagne flute and top up with the Champagne. Decorate with a lemon twist and serve.

COTTER KIR

ice cubes
2 teaspoons crème de cassis
2 teaspoons crème de framboise
1 measure cranberry juice
3 measures rosé wine
3 measures soda water
raspberries, to decorate

Fill a wine glass with ice cubes. Add the remaining ingredients and stir. Decorate with a couple of raspberries on a cocktail stick and serve.

GINNY GIN FIZZ

2 measures gin

I camomile tea bag

I measure sugar syrup

I measure lemon juice

3 teaspoons egg white

ice cubes

3 measures soda water

lemon twist, to decorate

Pour the gin into a cocktail shaker, add the tea bag and leave to infuse for 2 minutes.

Remove the tea bag and add the sugar syrup, lemon juice and egg white. Fill the shaker with ice cubes.

Shake and strain into a wine glass filled with ice cubes and top up with the soda water. Decorate with a lemon twist and serve.

LONG BLUSH

1 measure vodka
2 teaspoons clear honey
1 measure pomegranate juice
2 teaspoons lime juice
1 measure rosé wine
5 mint leaves
2 measures soda water
crushed ice

TO DECORATE
mint sprig
pomegranate seeds

Add the vodka, honey, pomegranate and lime juices, wine
and mint leaves to a cocktail shaker and shake.

Strain into a sling glass and add the soda water. Top up
the glass with crushed ice, decorate with a mint sprig and
some pomegranate seeds and serve.

PINK SANGRIA

3 measures rosé wine
2 teaspoons agave syrup
ice cubes
2 measures pomegranate juice
2 measures lemon verbena tea
2 measures soda water
pink grapefruit slice, to decorate

Pour the wine into a wine glass, add I teaspoon of the agave syrup and stir until it dissolves.

Fill the glass up with ice cubes and add the remaining agave syrup, the pomegranate juice, lemon verbena tea and soda water. Decorate with a slice of pink grapefruit and serve.

PASSIONATA

1½ measures vodka
2 measures cranberry juice
1 passion fruit, halved
ice cubes
energy drink, to top up

Pour the vodka and cranberry juice into a highball glass.
Scoop out the flesh from one half of the passion fruit and
add this to the glass. Add several ice cubes to the glass and
stir until well combined.

Top up the glass with the energy drink, decorate with the
other half of the passion fruit and serve.

VIBE ALIVE

2 grapefruit wedges

2 lime wedges

I teaspoon orgeat syrup

I½ measures gin

ice cubes

energy drink, to top up

Put the grapefruit and lime wedges and the orgeat syrup into a highball glass and muddle together. Pour the gin into the glass and stir well.

Add several ice cubes, top up with the energy drink, stir well and serve with a straw.

THE MIDWEEK SLUMP

EARLY NIGHT

2 tablespoons lemon juice
2 measures clear honey
2 measures whisky
4 measures boiling water
2 measures ginger wine
lemon slices, to decorate

Put the lemon juice and honey into 2 toddy glasses and
stir well. Add the whisky and continue stirring. Stir in the
boiling water, then add the ginger wine.

Decorate each glass with lemon slices. Serve at once
and drink while still hot.

NORTH POLE

2 measures gin
1 measure lemon juice
1 measure maraschino liqueur
2 egg whites
ice cubes

Put the gin, lemon juice, maraschino and egg whites into
a cocktail shaker, add 8–10 ice cubes and shake well.

Strain into 2 martini glasses and serve.

BEDTIME BOUNCER

4 measures brandy

2 measures Cointreau

10 measures bitter lemon

ice cubes

lemon spirals, to decorate

Pour the brandy, Cointreau and bitter lemon into a mixing glass and stir well.

Put 8–12 ice cubes into 2 highball glasses and pour the brandy mixture over the ice. Decorate each glass with lemon spirals and serve with straws.

CUCUMBER SAKE-TINI

ice cubes
5 measures cucumber-infused sake
3 measures gin
1 measure Curaçao
cucumber slices, to decorate

Put some ice cubes into a mixing glass with the sake,
gin and Curaçao and stir until thoroughly chilled.

Strain into 2 chilled martini glasses. Decorate each glass
with cucumber slices and serve.

SURF RIDER

ice cubes
6 measures vodka
2 measures sweet vermouth
juice of 1 lemon
juice of 2 oranges
1 teaspoon grenadine

Put 8–10 ice cubes into a cocktail shaker. Pour the vodka, vermouth, fruit juices and grenadine over the ice and shake until a frost forms on the outside of the shaker.

Strain into 2 old-fashioned glasses and serve immediately.

MEXICAN BULLDOG

ice cubes
1½ measures tequila
1½ measures Kahlúa coffee liqueur
2½ measures single cream
7 measures cola
drinking chocolate powder, to decorate

Put 4–6 ice cubes in 2 highball glasses. Pour in the tequila,
Kahlúa and cream, then top up with the cola.

Stir gently, sprinkle with drinking chocolate
powder and serve.

B-52

1 measure Kahlúa coffee liqueur
1 measure Bailey's Irish Cream
1 measure Grand Marnier

Pour the Kahlúa into 2 shot glasses. Using the back of a bar spoon, slowly float the Bailey's over the Kahlúa to form a separate layer.

Layer the Grand Marnier over the Bailey's in the same way and serve.

CLOUDY COOLER

5 white grapes, plus 1 extra, halved, to decorate

4 measures white wine

2 measures cloudy apple juice

1 teaspoon passion fruit syrup

ice cubes

2 measures soda water

pear slice, to decorate

Muddle the grapes in the bottom of a cocktail shaker. Add the wine, apple juice and passion fruit syrup and shake.

Strain into a highball glass full of ice cubes and top up with soda water. Decorate with a pear slice and a grape, halved, on a cocktail stick and serve.

SCOTCH GINGER HIGHBALL

ice cubes
2 measures Scotch whisky
1 measure lemon juice
3 teaspoons sugar syrup
4 measures ginger ale
mint sprigs, to decorate

Pour the whisky, lemon juice, sugar syrup and ginger
ale into a highball glass filled with ice cubes and stir.
Decorate with mint sprigs and serve.

MANDARIN 75

3 teaspoons mandarin oleo-saccharum (see tip)
1 measure chilled orange juice
4 measures chilled Champagne
orange twist, to decorate

Add the oleo-saccharum to a Champagne flute, pour in the orange juice and Champagne and stir gently. Decorate with an orange twist on a cocktail stick and serve.

TIP

OLEO-SACCHARUM IS A SYRUP PRODUCED FROM THE OIL OF CITRUS RIND AND SUGAR. TO MAKE MANDARIN OLEO-SACCHARUM, WASH 1 MANDARIN, THEN USE A VEGETABLE PEELER TO PEEL THE RIND FROM THE FRUIT, REMOVING AS LITTLE WHITE PITH AS POSSIBLE. PLACE THE RIND IN A SMALL BOWL, ADD 3 TABLESPOONS CASTER SUGAR AND PRESS THE SUGAR AND RIND FIRMLY WITH A MUDDLER UNTIL THE RIND BEGINS TO EXPRESS OILS. ALLOW THE MIXTURE TO SIT AT ROOM TEMPERATURE FOR AN HOUR UNTIL THE SUGAR HAS DISSOLVED.

RISING SUN

ice cubes
4 measures vodka
4 teaspoons passion fruit syrup
6 measures grapefruit juice
pink grapefruit slices, to decorate

Half-fill a cocktail shaker with ice cubes and put 6–8 ice
cubes into each old-fashioned glass.

Add all the remaining ingredients to the shaker and shake
until a frost forms on the outside of the shaker.

Strain into the glasses, decorate each with a pink grapefruit
slice and serve.

PINK COOLER

5 watermelon chunks, plus extra to decorate
2 measures lemon vodka
ice cubes
2 measures bitter lemon

Muddle the watermelon in the bottom of a cocktail shaker.
Add the vodka and shake.

Strain into an old-fashioned glass full of ice cubes and top
up with the bitter lemon. Decorate with a chunk of
watermelon and serve.

KIWI SMASH

½ kiwi fruit, quartered, plus an extra slice to decorate

4 lemon slices

4 teaspoons sugar syrup

2 measures gin

1 sprig coriander

crushed ice

Add the kiwi fruit, lemon slices and sugar syrup to an old-fashioned glass and muddle. Add the gin and coriander and half-fill the glass with crushed ice.

Churn with the muddler until thoroughly mixed. Top up with more crushed ice, decorate with a kiwi fruit slice on a cocktail stick and serve.

BETSY

2 measures gin or vodka

4 teaspoons lime juice

1 measure sugar syrup

2 strawberries, plus extra to decorate

1 sprig coriander

1 cup ice cubes

Put all the ingredients into a food processor or blender
and blend until smooth.

Pour into 2 old-fashioned glasses, decorate each with
a strawberry and serve.

CAPRISSIMA DA UVA

½ lime, plus a lime slice to decorate

5 red grapes, plus extra to decorate

2 measures amber rum

2 teaspoons caster sugar

2 teaspoons velvet falernum

crushed ice

Muddle the lime and grapes at the bottom of an old-fashioned glass. Add the rum, sugar and velvet falernum and half-fill the glass with crushed ice.

Churn the mixture with a muddler until thoroughly mixed. Top the glass up with more crushed ice, decorate with a lime slice and grape and serve.

HOPPER'S FIX

1½ measures dark rum
I measure espresso (cooled to room temperature or chilled)
½ teaspoon chocolate hazelnut spread
ice cubes
3 coffee beans, to decorate

Put the rum, espresso and chocolate hazelnut spread into
a cocktail shaker. Muddle the ingredients well in order
to dissolve the chocolate hazelnut chocolate spread.
Add several ice cubes and shake well until a frost forms
on the outside of the shaker.

Strain into a martini glass. Decorate with the coffee beans
floated in a cluster on the surface and serve.

ST CLEMENTS COLLINS

I½ measures white rum

I citrus tea bag

ice cubes

2 teaspoons lemon juice

I teaspoon caster sugar

soda water, to top up

orange or lemon twist, to decorate

Pour the rum into a wine glass, add the tea bag and leave to steep for 2 minutes.

Remove the tea bag and add some ice cubes to the glass. Add the remaining ingredients and stir. Decorate with a twist of orange or lemon and serve.

PINEAPPLE JULEP

1½ measures bourbon

10 mint leaves

2 teaspoons cardamom syrup (see tip)

2 measures pineapple juice

crushed ice

pineapple leaves, to decorate

Add the bourbon, mint leaves, cardamom syrup and pineapple juice to a julep tin or jam jar and churn together with a muddler.

Fill the tin or jam jar with crushed ice, decorate with pineapple leaves and serve with a straw.

TIP

TO MAKE THE CARDAMOM SYRUP, STEEP 20 CARDAMOM PODS IN 500 ML (17 FL OZ) SUGAR SYRUP FOR 48 HOURS, AND STRAIN.

SOMETHING FOR
THE WEEKEND

SOUTH FOR THE SUMMER

4 teaspoons grenadine
4 measures tequila
6 measures orange juice
8 fresh pineapple chunks
crushed ice

TO DECORATE
pineapple leaves
orange spirals

Pour the grenadine gently into 2 highball glasses.

Put the tequila, orange juice and pineapple chunks into a food processor or blender with some crushed ice and blend until slushy.

Pour the mixture over the grenadine. Decorate each glass with a pineapple leaf and an orange spiral and stir just before serving.

BUCK'S TWIZZ

2 measures chilled orange juice
1 measure maraschino liqueur
2 measures Absolut Mandarin vodka
chilled Champagne, to top up
rindless pink grapefruit slices, to decorate

Pour the orange juice and maraschino into 2 chilled
Champagne saucers.

Add the vodka and Champagne at the same time
(this prevents excessive fizzing). Decorate each glass
with a rindless pink grapefruit slice and serve.

GRASSHOPPER

2 measures white crème de cacao
2 measures crème de menthe
mint sprigs, to decorate

Pour the crème de cacao into 2 martini glasses.

Using the back of a bar spoon, slowly float the crème de menthe over the crème de cacao to form a separate layer. Decorate each glass with mint sprigs and serve.

POPPY

ice cubes
1½ measures vodka
2 dashes Chambord
2 teaspoons pineapple purée

Put some ice cubes into a cocktail shaker, add the vodka,
Chambord and pineapple purée and shake briefly.

Strain into 2 shot glasses and serve.

TIJUANA MARY

4 watermelon chunks, plus a watermelon wedge to decorate
2 measures tequila
2 teaspoons sriracha sauce
1 pinch salt
2 pinches pink peppercorns
ice cubes
4 measures tomato juice

Place the watermelon chunks in a cocktail shaker and muddle.
Add the tequila, sriracha sauce, salt, peppercorns and some ice
cubes and shake.

Strain into a Collins glass full of ice cubes and top up with the
tomato juice. Stir well, decorate with a watermelon wedge and serve.

ROSSINI

4 strawberries

2 teaspoons sugar syrup

5 measures chilled prosecco

Put the strawberries and sugar syrup into a food processor
or blender and blend until smooth.

Strain into a Champagne flute, top up with the prosecco and serve.

PRIMROSE FIZZ

4 mint leaves
ice cubes
4 teaspoons elderflower liqueur
I measure apple juice
4 measures chilled Champagne
apple slice, to decorate

Bruise the mint leaves and then place them in a small wine glass.

Fill the glass with ice cubes, add the remaining ingredients and stir.
Decorate with an apple slice and serve.

WATERMELON SMASH

I measure tequila

4 watermelon chunks

5 mint leaves, plus an extra sprig to decorate

I teaspoon agave syrup

I cup crushed ice

Add all the ingredients to a food processor or blender and blend until smooth.

Pour into an old-fashioned glass, decorate with a mint sprig and serve.

ABC COCKTAIL

ice cubes

I measure VSOP Cognac

I measure tawny port

2 teaspoons maraschino liqueur

6 mint leaves, plus extra to decorate

Add all the ingredients to a cocktail shaker and shake.

Strain into a martini glass, decorate with a mint leaf and serve.

WILLIAM'S PEAR

½ ripe pear, cut into chunks, plus pear slices to decorate

3 teaspoons redcurrant jam

2 measures bourbon

4 teaspoons lemon juice

2 teaspoons sugar syrup

ice cubes

Muddle the pear and jam in the bottom of a cocktail
shaker. Add the remaining ingredients and shake.

Strain into an old-fashioned glass full of ice cubes,
decorate with pear slices and serve.

TURF

crushed ice
2 measures gin
2 measures dry vermouth
2 teaspoons lemon juice
2 teaspoons Pernod
lemon slices, to decorate

Put some crushed ice into a cocktail shaker. Pour the gin, vermouth, lemon juice and Pernod over the ice and shake well.

Strain into 2 highball glasses filled with crushed ice. Decorate each glass with a lemon slice and serve with straws.

SWEET & CHILLI

3 measures Scotch whisky

1½ measures blood orange juice

1½ measures Antica Formula or sweet vermouth

2 teaspoons agave syrup

ice cubes

red chillies, about 2.5 cm (1 inch) long, to decorate

Add the whisky, blood orange juice, Antica Formula or vermouth
and agave syrup to a cocktail shaker with some ice cubes and
shake well until a frost forms on the outside of the shaker.

Strain into 2 frozen coupette or margarita glasses (see tip),
decorate each with a chilli and serve.

TIP

**TO FREEZE A GLASS, PLACE IN THE FREEZER FOR ABOUT
10–15 MINUTES.**

PIMM'S CUCUMBER RANGOON

ice cubes

2 measures Pimm's No. 1 Cup

2 measures cucumber juice (see tip)

3½ measures ginger ale

TO DECORATE

cucumber strips

orange slices

blueberries

Pour all the ingredients into a Collins glass filled with ice cubes. Stir well, decorate with cucumber strips twisted around the edge of the glass, orange slices and blueberries, and serve with a straw.

TIP

TO MAKE CUCUMBER JUICE, PEEL A CUCUMBER AND THEN PROCESS IT IN A BLENDER OR JUICER. STRAIN THE JUICE BEFORE USE.

BLUEBERRY JULEP POPTAILS

125 g (4 oz) caster sugar
4 sprigs mint
225 g (7½ oz) blueberries
6 tablespoons bourbon

Place the sugar and mint in a saucepan with 250 ml (8 fl oz) water and slowly bring to the boil, allowing the sugar to dissolve. Simmer gently for 5 minutes, then remove from the heat and allow the syrup to infuse for 30 minutes.

Place the blueberries and bourbon in a food processor or blender and pour over the syrup, mint sprigs included. Blitz until completely smooth. Pour into 6 popsicle moulds.

Place the moulds in the freezer for 2 hours. Insert the popsicle sticks and return to the freezer until frozen solid, about 4 more hours.

CARDAMOM POPTAILS

1 green tea bag	50 g (2 oz) caster sugar
125 ml (4 fl oz) boiling water	6 tablespoons whisky
4 cardamom pods	500 g (1 lb) plain yogurt

Place the tea bag in a jug and pour over the boiling water. Set aside
and leave to infuse for 10 minutes. Discard the tea bag.

Using a mortar and pestle, lightly crush the cardamom pods. Place
the crushed cardamom pods and sugar in a saucepan. Pour over the
green tea and let the sugar dissolve, then bring to a simmer and allow
to bubble for 10 minutes, until you have a thick syrup. Combine the
syrup with the whisky.

Put the yogurt into a mixing bowl, then stir through the whisky syrup.
Pour into 6 popsicle moulds.

Place the moulds in the freezer. Freeze for 1 hour, then insert the
popsicle sticks and return to the freezer until frozen solid, about
2 more hours.

ENGLISH SUMMER CUP POPTAILS

50 g (2 oz) caster sugar
4 tablespoons Pimm's No. 1 Cup
250 ml (8 fl oz) ginger beer or lemonade
150 g (5 oz) strawberries, sliced
50 g (2 oz) apples, sliced
18 small mint leaves

Place the sugar and 125 ml (4 fl oz) water in a saucepan and slowly bring to the boil, allowing the sugar to dissolve. Simmer gently for 5 minutes, then remove from the heat, add the Pimm's and ginger beer or lemonade and allow to cool completely.

Divide the strawberries, apple slices and mint leaves among 6 popsicle moulds. Pour over the Pimm's mixture and insert the popsicle sticks.

Place the moulds in the freezer until frozen solid, about 6 hours.

EL DIABLO ICE CREAMS

500 ml (17 fl oz) milk
250 ml (8 fl oz) double cream
1 chilli, chopped (optional)
250 g (8 oz) chocolate, chopped

4 measures rum
2 egg yolks
50 g (2 oz) caster sugar

Place the milk, cream and chilli, if using, in a saucepan and bring to the boil. Remove from the heat and leave to stand for 5 minutes. Place the chocolate in a heatproof bowl, pour the milk mixture over it, and stir until the chocolate has melted. Stir in the rum.

Whisk the egg yolks and sugar in a bowl and gradually pour over the chocolate mixture, whisking all the time, until well combined. Cover the surface with plastic wrap and allow to cool completely.

Place the mixture in an ice cream machine and churn according to the manufacturer's instructions. Alternatively, place the mixture in a covered container in the freezer and beat it every 30 minutes to get rid of any graininess. Keep freezing and beating until it becomes a smooth ice cream consistency.

Pack 8 popsicle moulds with the ice cream. Insert the popsicle sticks and freeze until solid, about 4 hours.

NECTARINE & BASIL ICE CREAMS

175 g (6 oz) chopped nectarines
50 g (2 oz) caster sugar
8 tablespoons basil leaves
500 ml (17 fl oz) vanilla ice cream
4 measures vodka

Place the nectarines, sugar and half the basil leaves in a saucepan with 2 tablespoons water. Slowly bring to the boil and cook until the nectarines are completely soft, about 15 minutes. Remove from the heat, transfer to a food processor or blender and blitz until completely smooth. Allow the nectarine purée to cool completely.

Meanwhile, remove the ice cream from the freezer and let soften for 20 minutes. Place in a large bowl.

Coarsely chop the remaining basil leaves. In a small bowl, combine the nectarine purée, chopped basil leaves and vodka, then stir into the softened ice cream.

Pack 8 popsicle moulds with the ice cream. Insert the popsicle sticks and freeze until solid, about 2 hours.

PARTY TIME

VALENCIAN SANGRIA

ice cubes
1 measure brandy
2 measures blood orange juice
1 pinch pink peppercorns
1 measure sweet vermouth
2 teaspoons Campari
2 measures red wine
2 measures soda water
orange slice, to decorate

Fill a wine glass with ice cubes. Add all the remaining ingredients and stir.

Decorate with an orange slice and serve.

CHAMPAGNE JULEP

4 mint sprigs, plus extra to decorate
2 tablespoons sugar syrup
crushed ice
2 measures brandy
chilled Champagne, to top up

Put the mint sprigs and sugar syrup into 2 highball glasses
and muddle together.

Fill the glasses with crushed ice, then add the brandy.
Top up with Champagne and stir gently. Decorate each
glass with mint sprigs and serve.

RITZ FIZZ

2 dashes blue Curaçao
2 dashes lemon juice
2 dashes Amaretto di Saronno
chilled Champagne, to top up
lemon spirals, to decorate

Pour the Curaçao, lemon juice and Amaretto into a mixing glass and mix together.

Transfer to 2 Champagne flutes and top up with Champagne. Stir gently to mix, decorate each glass with a lemon spiral and serve.

VODKA SAZERAC

2 sugar cubes

4 drops Angostura bitters

5 drops Pernod

6–8 ice cubes

4 measures vodka

lemonade, to top up

Put the sugar cubes in 2 old-fashioned glasses and shake the bitters on top.

Add the Pernod and swirl it around to coat the inside of each glass.

Drop in the ice cubes and pour in the vodka. Top up with lemonade, stir gently to mix and serve.

GLÖGG

2 bottles dry red wine or 1 bottle
red wine and 1 bottle port or Madeira

rind of 1 orange

20 cardamom pods, lightly crushed

2 cinnamon sticks

20 whole cloves

175 g (6 oz) blanched almonds

250 g (8 oz) raisins

250–375 g (8–12 oz) sugar cubes

300 ml (½ pint) Aquavit or brandy

Put the wine or wine and port or Madeira into a saucepan. Tie the orange rind
and spices in a piece of muslin and add to the pan. Add the almonds and raisins.
Heat at just below boiling point for 25 minutes, stirring occasionally.

Put a wire rack over the pan and put the sugar cubes on it. Warm the Aquavit
or brandy and pour it over the sugar cubes to saturate them evenly. Set them
alight: they will melt through the wire rack into the wine.

Stir the glögg and remove the spice bag. Serve hot, putting a few raisins and
almonds in each cup.

MAKES **2** * GLASSES 2 warmed martini glasses
EQUIPMENT bar spoon, 2 shot glasses, warmed wine glass, straws

FLAMING LAMBORGHINI

2 measures Kahlúa coffee liqueur
2 measures Sambuca
2 measures Bailey's Irish Cream
2 measures blue Curaçao

Pour the Kahlúa into 2 warmed martini glasses. Using the back of a bar spoon, slowly float half a measure of Sambuca over the Kahlúa to form a separate layer.

Pour the Bailey's and Curaçao into shot glasses.

Next, pour the remaining Sambuca into a warmed wine glass and carefully set it alight. Carefully pour it into the martini glasses.

Pour the Bailey's and Curaçao into the lighted martini glasses at the same time. Serve with straws.

TEQUILA SLAMMER

2 measures tequila gold
2 measures chilled Champagne

Pour the tequila into 2 shot glasses. Slowly top up with the Champagne.

Cover the top of the glass with the palm of your hand to seal the contents inside and grip it with your fingers. Briskly pick up the glass and slam it down on a surface to make the drink fizz. Quickly gulp it down in one, while it's still fizzing.

FIREBALL

1 measure absinthe

1 measure ice-cold kümmel

1 measure Goldschläger

Pour the absinthe into 2 shot glasses. Using the back of a bar spoon, slowly float the kümmel over the absinthe to form a separate layer.

Layer the Goldschläger over the kümmel in the same way and serve.

LOS ALTOS

5 slices tangerine

3 teaspoons agave syrup

2 measures tequila

2 teaspoons lime juice

2 teaspoons Campari

ice cubes

4 measures soda water

TO DECORATE

orange slice

lime slice

Add the tangerine slices and agave syrup to a cocktail shaker and muddle. Pour in the tequila, lime juice and Campari and shake.

Strain into a Collins glass filled with ice cubes and top up with the soda water. Decorate with an orange slice and a lime slice and serve.

RIVIERA FIZZ

3 measures sloe gin
1 measure lemon juice
1 measure sugar syrup
ice cubes
chilled Champagne, to top up
lemon twists, to decorate

Pour the sloe gin, lemon juice and sugar syrup into
a cocktail shaker and add some ice cubes.

Shake and strain into 2 chilled Champagne flutes. Top up
with Champagne, stir, decorate each glass with a lemon
twist and serve.

FRENCH PINK LADY

2 measures gin

4 raspberries

I measure Triple Sec

3 teaspoons lime juice

I teaspoon pastis

ice cubes

lime wedge, to decorate

Add the gin, raspberries, Triple Sec, lime juice and pastis to a cocktail shaker and muddle. Fill the shaker with ice cubes and shake.

Strain into a martini glass, decorate with a lime wedge and serve.

GIN TROPICAL

8 ice cubes

1½ measures gin

I measure lemon juice

I measure passion fruit juice

½ measure orange juice

soda water, to top up

orange spiral, to decorate

Put 4 of the ice cubes into a cocktail shaker, pour in the gin
and fruit juices and shake well.

Put 4 ice cubes into an old-fashioned glass and strain
the cocktail over the ice. Top up with soda water and stir
gently. Decorate with an orange spiral and serve.

SHERRY PUNCH

5 pineapple chunks
5 raspberries
3 lemon slices
2 teaspoons sugar syrup
2 measures fino sherry
crushed ice

TO DECORATE
pineapple wedge
raspberry

Add the pineapple chunks, raspberries, lemon slices and sugar syrup
to a cocktail shaker and muddle. Add the sherry and shake.

Strain into an old-fashioned glass full of crushed ice, decorate with
a pineapple wedge and a raspberry on a cocktail stick and serve.

DUKE'S DAIQUIRI

2 measures white rum

3 teaspoons lime juice

1 measure sugar syrup

tinned peach half, drained

1 measure cloudy apple juice

1 teaspoon grenadine

1 cup ice cubes

TO DECORATE

lime slice

black cherry

Add all ingredients to a food processor or blender and blend until smooth.

Pour into a hurricane glass, decorate with a lime slice and a cherry and serve.

COCONUT & LIME MARGARITA

ice cubes

3 measures 100 per cent agave tequila

4 teaspoons lime cordial

4 teaspoons coconut syrup

3 measures pineapple juice

1 measure lime juice

lime slices, to decorate

Combine the ingredients in a cocktail shaker and shake well until a frost forms on the outside of the shaker.

Strain into 2 martini glasses and decorate each with a lime slice.

TEQUILA SUNRISE POPTAILS

125 ml (4 fl oz) lemon juice
125 g (4 oz) caster sugar
4 tablespoons tequila

125 ml (4 fl oz) soda water
1 tablespoon crème de cassis

Place the lemon juice and sugar in a saucepan with 125 ml (4 fl oz) water and slowly bring to the boil, allowing the sugar to dissolve. Allow to simmer for 5 minutes, then remove from the heat.

Pour in the tequila and soda water and mix well to combine. Measure out 6 tablespoons of the mixture and set aside. Divide the remaining mixture among 6 popsicle moulds. Place the moulds in the freezer for 4 hours.

Combine the reserved mixture with the cassis. After the 4 hours are up (see tip), remove the lollies from the freezer and pour the cassis mixture into the moulds. Insert the popsicle sticks and freeze for another 4–6 hours, until frozen solid.

TIP
WHEN YOU POUR THE CASSIS MIXTURE INTO THE MOULDS YOU WANT IT TO
FLOAT ON TOP AND SLIGHTLY BLEND IN WITH THE TEQUILA BASE. SO THE
TEQUILA NEEDS TO BE ALMOST FROZEN, BUT STILL A LITTLE SLUSHY.

FLAMINGO-GO POPTAILS

125 g (4 oz) caster sugar
75 g (3 oz) pomegranate seeds (from 1 pomegranate – see tip)
250 ml (8 fl oz) prosecco
1 tablespoon rose water

Place the sugar and 250 ml (8 fl oz) water in a saucepan and slowly bring to the boil, allowing the sugar to dissolve. Allow to simmer for 5 minutes, then remove from the heat.

Stir in the pomegranate seeds, prosecco and rose water. Pour into 6 popsicle moulds.

Place the moulds in the freezer. After 3 hours give each one a gentle stir to distribute the pomegranate seeds and insert the popsicle sticks. Return to the freezer until frozen solid, about 3 more hours.

TIP
TO REMOVE THE SEEDS FROM THE POMEGRANATE, BASH IT WITH A WOODEN SPOON WHILE IT'S STILL WHOLE. THIS WILL LOOSEN THE SEEDS FROM THE SHELL AND MAKE THEM EASIER TO PICK OFF.

STRAWBERRY COSMOPOLITAN SLUSHIE

50 g (2 oz) caster sugar
200 g (7 oz) hulled and quartered strawberries
1 measure vodka
1 measure Cointreau
4½ measures soda water
lime slices, to decorate

Place the sugar and 125 ml (4 fl oz) water in a small saucepan. Let the sugar dissolve over a low heat, then bring the syrup to the boil. Remove from the heat.

Add the strawberries to the pan. Squash the strawberries into the syrup using the back of a fork or a pestle, but allowing some texture to remain. Pour in the remaining ingredients.

Pour the whole mixture into an ice cube tray. Freeze for 2 hours or until almost solid, then stir briefly to make a slush.

POMEGRANATE, VANILLA & VODKA ICE CUBES

½ vanilla pod
50 g (2 oz) caster sugar
350 ml (12 fl oz) pomegranate juice
65 ml (2 fl oz) vodka

Scrape the seeds from the vanilla pod and place both the pod and seeds in a saucepan with the sugar and 125 ml (5 fl oz) water. Slowly bring to the boil, allowing the sugar to dissolve, then simmer gently for 5 minutes. Remove from the heat and leave to infuse for 30 minutes.

Remove and discard the vanilla pod from the syrup. Mix in the pomegranate juice and vodka.

Pour into ice cube trays and place in the freezer. Let set for 2 hours or until slightly set before serving.

SWEET FIX

BRANDY CRUSTA

lemon wedges
caster sugar
4 measures brandy
I measure orange Curaçao
I measure maraschino liqueur
2 measures lemon juice
6 dashes Angostura bitters
ice cubes
lemon rind strips, to decorate

Dampen the rim of each chilled martini glass with a lemon
wedge, then dip into a saucer of caster sugar.

Put the brandy, Curaçao, maraschino, lemon juice and bitters into
a cocktail shaker with some ice cubes and shake well.

Strain into the prepared glasses, decorate each with lemon rind
strips and serve.

DAWA

2 limes, quartered and thickly sliced
2 tablespoons thick honey
2 teaspoons caster sugar
crushed ice
4 measures vodka

Put the lime slices, honey and sugar in 2 old-fashioned glasses
and muddle together.

Add some crushed ice, pour the vodka over the ice and serve.

GOOMBAY SMASH

3 measures coconut rum
2 measures cachaça
I measure apricot brandy
I measure lime juice
8 measures pineapple juice
ice cubes

TO DECORATE
pineapple wedges
lime twists
maraschino cherries

Put the rum, cachaça, brandy and fruit juices in a cocktail
shaker and add some ice cubes.

Shake and strain over more ice into 2 old-fashioned
glasses. Decorate each glass with a pineapple wedge, a lime
twist and some cherries on cocktail sticks and serve.

PLAYA DEL MAR

2 orange slices

light brown sugar and
sea salt, mixed

ice cubes

2½ measures tequila gold

1½ measures Grand Marnier

4 teaspoons lime juice

1½ measures cranberry juice

1½ measures pineapple juice

TO DECORATE

pineapple wedges

orange spirals

Dampen the rim of each highball glass with an orange slice, then dip into
a saucer of the sugar and salt mixture. Fill each glass with ice cubes.

Pour the tequila, Grand Marnier and fruit juices into a cocktail shaker.
Fill the shaker with ice cubes and shake vigorously for 10 seconds.

Strain into the prepared glasses. Decorate each glass with a pineapple
wedge and an orange spiral and serve.

MEXICAN MARSHMALLOW MOCHA

4 teaspoons cocoa powder, plus extra to decorate
2 measures Kahlúa coffee liqueur
7 measures hot filter coffee
mini marshmallows
whipped cream

Put 2 teaspoons cocoa powder into each toddy glass, add the Kahlúa and coffee and stir until mixed.

Drop in the mini marshmallows and float the cream on top. Decorate with cocoa powder and serve.

PUDDING COCKTAIL

2 measures Calvados

3 measures brandy

2 egg yolks

2 teaspoons caster sugar

ice cubes

ground cinnamon, to decorate

Put the Calvados, brandy, egg yolks and caster sugar into a cocktail shaker with some ice cubes and shake until well mixed.

Strain into 2 chilled martini glasses. Light a long taper, hold it over each glass in turn and sprinkle cinnamon through the flame on to the surface of the drink. Serve at once.

TIKI TREAT

crushed ice

1 ripe mango, peeled and stoned, plus extra slices to decorate

6 coconut chunks

2 measures coconut cream

4 measures aged rum

2 dashes lemon juice

2 teaspoons caster sugar

Put a small scoop of crushed ice with all the other ingredients into a food processor or blender and blend until smooth.

Pour into 2 hurricane glasses, decorate each glass with mango slices and serve with straws.

AFTER DARK CRUSH

crushed ice
4 measures Barbadian rum
1 measure Koko Kanu (coconut rum)
1 measure vanilla syrup
2 measures coconut cream
soda water, to top up
maraschino cherries, to decorate

Fill 2 highball glasses with crushed ice, then add, one by one
in order, the two rums, vanilla syrup and coconut cream.

Stir and top up with soda water. Add more ice, decorate with
cherries on cocktail sticks and serve with straws.

ZOOM

ice cubes
4 measures Scotch whisky
2 teaspoons clear honey
2 measures chilled water
2 measures single cream

Put 8–10 ice cubes into a cocktail shaker, add the whisky,
honey, chilled water and cream and shake well.

Strain into 2 old-fashioned glasses and serve at once.

ALEXANDER BABY

8–10 ice cubes

4 measures dark rum

2 measures crème de cacao

1 measure double cream

grated nutmeg, to decorate

Put the ice cubes into a cocktail shaker, add the rum, crème de cacao and cream and shake well.

Strain into 2 chilled martini glasses. Sprinkle a little grated nutmeg over each glass and serve.

DEAF KNEES

1 measure chocolate schnapps
1 measure crème de menthe
1 measure Grand Marnier

Pour the schnapps into 2 shot glasses. Using the back of a bar spoon, slowly float the crème de menthe over the schnapps to form a separate layer.

Layer the Grand Marnier over the crème de menthe in the same way and serve.

JAFFA

ice cubes
2 measures brandy
2 measures dark crème de cacao
2 measures single cream
1 measure Mandarine Napoléon
4 dashes orange bitters
orange-flavoured chocolate shavings, to decorate

Half-fill a cocktail shaker with ice cubes. Add the
remaining ingredients and shake until a frost forms on
the outside of the shaker.

Strain into 2 chilled martini glasses, decorate with
orange-flavoured chocolate shavings and serve.

PISCO PUNCH

2 measures pisco
2 pineapple chunks
1 measure orange juice
4 teaspoons lime juice
2 teaspoons falernum
2 teaspoons sugar syrup
2 dashes Angostura bitters
ice cubes
pineapple wedge, to decorate

Add all the ingredients to a cocktail shaker and muddle.

Shake, then strain into a wine glass filled with ice cubes.
Decorate with a pineapple wedge and serve.

CROSSBOW

drinking chocolate powder
4–5 ice cubes
I tablespoon gin
I tablespoon white crème de cacao
15 ml (½ fl oz) Cointreau

Dampen the rim of a chilled martini glass with a little
water, then dip into a saucer of drinking chocolate.

Put the ice cubes into a cocktail shaker and add the gin,
crème de cacao and Cointreau. Shake vigorously,
strain into the prepared glass and serve.

LEMON DROP

ice cubes
1½ measures lemon vodka
1½ measures limoncello
1 dash lemon juice
1 dash lime cordial

Put some ice cubes into a cocktail shaker, add the vodka,
limoncello, lemon juice and lime cordial and shake briefly.

Strain into 2 shot glasses and serve.

GOLDEN APRICOT

3 tablespoons rum

3 teaspoons apricot liqueur

4 teaspoons lime juice

4 teaspoons sugar syrup

I egg yolk

ice cubes

4 measures soda water

dried apricot, to decorate

Put the rum, apricot liqueur, lime juice, sugar syrup and egg yolk into a food processor or blender and blend.

Strain into a Collins glass and fill the glass with ice cubes before topping up with the soda water. Decorate with a dried apricot on a cocktail stick and serve with a straw.

VALENTINE MARTINI

ice cubes

4 measures raspberry vodka

12 raspberries, plus extra to decorate

1 measure lime juice

2 dashes sugar syrup

lime spirals, to decorate

Half-fill a cocktail shaker with ice cubes. Add all the remaining ingredients and shake until a frost forms on the outside of the shaker.

Double-strain into 2 chilled martini glasses. Decorate each glass with raspberries and lime spirals on cocktail sticks and serve.

PASSION FRUIT MARGARITA POPTAILS

125 g (4 oz) caster sugar
grated rind of 1 lime
125 ml (4 fl oz) passion fruit
pulp (about 6 passion fruit)

3 measures lime juice
1 measure tequila
½ measure Cointreau

Place the sugar and lime rind in a small saucepan with 250 ml (8 fl oz) water. Slowly bring to the boil, allowing the sugar to dissolve. Allow to simmer for 5 minutes, then remove from the heat.

Stir in the remaining ingredients and pour into 6 popsicle moulds.

Place the moulds in the freezer. After 3 hours give each one a gentle stir to distribute the passion fruit seeds and insert the popsicle sticks. Return to the freezer until frozen solid, about 3 more hours.

TIP

WHEN REMOVING THE SEEDS FROM THE PASSION FRUIT, BE SURE NOT TO LOSE ANY OF THE DELICIOUS JUICE.

WATERMELON PUNCH

1 watermelon (about 9 kg/20 lb)
200 ml (7 fl oz) vodka
20 mint leaves
3 measures lemon juice
5 measures sugar syrup
1 cup ice cubes
lemon slice, to decorate

Cut the top off the watermelon and use a spoon to scoop out the flesh inside. Set aside the hollowed-out watermelon.

Remove the pips from the watermelon flesh, then add the flesh and the remaining ingredients to a food processor or blender and blend until smooth.

Pour into the hollowed-out watermelon, decorate with a lemon slice and serve with straws.

CAN'T GO WRONG
WITH A CLASSIC

MOJITO

16 mint leaves, plus sprigs to decorate

1 lime, cut into wedges

4 teaspoons cane sugar

crushed ice

5 measures white rum

soda water, to top up

Muddle the mint leaves, lime and sugar in the bottom
of 2 highball glasses and fill with crushed ice.

Add the rum, stir and top up with soda water.
Decorate each glass with mint sprigs and serve.

LONG ISLAND ICED TEA

I measure vodka

I measure gin

I measure white rum

I measure tequila

I measure Cointreau

I measure lemon juice

ice cubes

cola, to top up

lemon slices, to decorate

Put the vodka, gin, rum, tequila, Cointreau and lemon juice in a cocktail shaker with some ice cubes and shake to mix.

Strain into 2 highball glasses filled with ice cubes and top up with cola. Decorate each glass with lemon slices and serve.

MARGARITA

2 lime wedges
rock salt
4 measures Herradura Reposado tequila
2 measures lime juice
2 measures Triple Sec
ice cubes
lime slices, to decorate

Dampen the rim of each coupette or margarita glass with a
lime wedge, then dip it into a saucer of rock salt.

Pour the tequila, lime juice and Triple Sec into a cocktail shaker,
add some ice cubes and shake.

Strain into the prepared glasses, decorate each with a slice
of lime and serve.

RUSTY NAIL

ice cubes
3 measures Scotch whisky
2 measures Drambuie

Fill 2 old-fashioned glasses with ice cubes. Pour the
whisky and Drambuie over the ice and serve.

WHITE RUSSIAN

12 cracked ice cubes
2 measures vodka
2 measures Tia Maria
2 measures full-fat milk or double cream

Put half the cracked ice into a cocktail shaker and put the remaining cracked ice into 2 old-fashioned glasses. Add the vodka, Tia Maria and milk or cream to the shaker and shake until a frost forms on the outside of the shaker.

Strain over the ice in the glasses and serve.

SEA BREEZE

ice cubes
2 measures vodka
4 measures cranberry juice
2 measures grapefruit juice
lemon rind strips, to decorate

Fill 2 highball glasses with ice cubes, pour over the vodka and fruit juices and stir well. Decorate each glass with lemon rind strips and serve.

SEX ON THE BEACH

ice cubes
2 measures vodka
2 measures peach schnapps
2 measures cranberry juice
2 measures orange juice
2 measures pineapple juice (optional)

TO DECORATE
lemon wedges
lime wedges

Put 8–10 ice cubes into a cocktail shaker and add the vodka, schnapps, cranberry juice, orange juice and pineapple juice (if using). Shake well.

Put 3–4 ice cubes into each highball glass, strain over the cocktail and decorate each with the lemon and lime wedges.

CUBA LIBRE

ice cubes
2 measures golden rum, such as Havana Club 3-year-old
juice of ½ lime
cola, to top up
lime wedges, to decorate

Fill an old-fashioned or highball glass with ice cubes. Pour over the rum and lime juice and stir.

Top up with cola, decorate with lime wedges and serve with a straw.

CAN'T GO WRONG WITH A CLASSIC

TOM COLLINS

2 measures gin

I measure sugar syrup

I measure lemon juice

ice cubes

4 measures soda water

TO DECORATE

lemon wedge

black cherry

Pour the gin, sugar syrup and lemon juice into a cocktail shaker and fill with ice cubes.

Shake, then strain into a Collins glass full of ice cubes and top up with the soda water. Decorate with a lemon wedge and a cherry and serve.

WHISKY HIGHBALL

ice cubes

2 measures Scotch whisky

I dash Angostura bitters

4 measures soda water

lemon twist, to decorate

Add 3 large ice cubes and the whisky and bitters to a highball glass.

Stir gently, then fill the glass with more ice cubes and top up with the soda water. Decorate with a lemon twist and serve.

SINGAPORE SLING

ice cubes

2 measures gin

1 measure cherry brandy

½ measure Cointreau

½ measure Bénédictine

1 measure grenadine

1 measure lime juice

10 measures pineapple juice

1–2 dashes Angostura bitters

TO DECORATE

pineapple wedges

maraschino cherries

Half-fill a cocktail shaker with ice cubes and put some ice cubes into each highball glass. Add the remaining ingredients to the shaker and shake until a frost forms on the outside of the shaker.

Strain over the ice cubes in the glasses. Decorate each glass with a pineapple wedge and a maraschino cherry on a cocktail stick and serve.

BELLINI

½ ripe white peach
2 teaspoons sugar syrup
5 measures chilled prosecco

Put the peach and sugar syrup into a food processor or blender
and blend until smooth.

Strain into a Champagne flute, top with the prosecco and serve.

WHISKY SOUR

ice cubes
2 measures Scotch whisky
1 measure lemon juice
1 measure sugar syrup

TO DECORATE
lemon wedge
lemon spirals

Fill a cocktail shaker with ice cubes. Add the remaining
ingredients and shake.

Strain into an old-fashioned glass filled with ice cubes,
decorate with a lemon wedge and a lemon spiral and serve.

DAIQUIRI

ice cubes
2 measures light rum
I measure sugar syrup
I measure lime juice
lime wedge, to decorate

Add all the ingredients to a cocktail shaker and shake.

Strain into a martini glass, decorate with a lime wedge and serve.

OLD-FASHIONED

ice cubes
2 measures bourbon
I teaspoon sugar syrup
I dash orange bitters
I dash Angostura bitters
orange twist, to decorate

Half-fill an old-fashioned glass with ice cubes. Add the remaining ingredients to the glass and stir for I minute.

Fill the glass with more ice cubes. Decorate with an orange twist and serve.

CLASSIC MARTINI

ice cubes
1 measure dry vermouth
6 measures gin
stuffed green olives, to decorate

Put 10–12 ice cubes into a mixing glass. Pour over the vermouth and gin and stir (never shake) vigorously and evenly without splashing.

Strain into 2 chilled martini glasses, decorate each with a green olive on a cocktail stick and serve.

NEGRONI

ice cubes
1 measure gin
1 measure sweet vermouth
1 measure Campari
orange wedge, to decorate

Fill an old-fashioned glass with ice cubes, add the remaining ingredients and stir. Decorate with an orange wedge and serve.

COSMOPOLITAN

ice cubes
1½ measures lemon vodka
4 teaspoons Triple Sec
3 teaspoons lime juice
I measure cranberry juice
lime slice, to decorate

Add all the ingredients to a cocktail shaker and shake.

Strain into a martini glass, decorate with a slice of lime and serve.

GODMOTHER

cracked ice cubes

3 measures vodka

1 measure Amaretto di Saronno

Put 2–3 cracked ice cubes into each old-fashioned glass.
Add the vodka and Amaretto, stir lightly to mix and serve.

CAIPIRINHA

6 lime wedges

2 teaspoons brown sugar

2 measures cachaça

crushed ice

Place 3 lime wedges in a large tumbler or old-fashioned glass and add the brown sugar and cachaça. Mix well, mashing the limes slightly to make a little juice.

Top up with crushed ice, decorate with the remaining lime wedges and serve.

INDEX

ACKNOWLEDGEMENTS

Senior Commissioning Editor: Eleanor Maxfield
Editor: Natalie Bradley
Design: Jaz Bahra
Production Controller: Denise Woolery

PICTURE CREDITS

Getty Images John Carey 300; Alexandra Grablewski 33, 51, 148, 151; Jim Jurica 24; Niki van Velden
81. **iStock** Paul Johnson 244; Wiktory 274. **Octopus Publishing Group** Stephen Conroy 9, 17, 18,
21, 23, 27, 28, 30, 42, 44, 59, 61, 62, 65, 66, 68, 71, 72, 88, 91, 93, 97, 99, 100, 103, 104, 107, 109, 110,
112, 135, 136, 138, 141, 142, 145, 147, 154, 173, 175, 178, 178, 212, 215, 216, 219, 221, 222, 225, 229,
251, 253, 254, 256, 259, 260, 263, 265, 266, 271, 273, 279, 282, 290, 292, 295, 297, 298, 303, 304, 310,
321, 326, 328; Jonathan Kennedy 13, 34, 36, 39, 41, 47, 48, 54, 75, 76, 78, 82, 85, 87, 115, 116, 119, 120,
122, 125, 127, 128, 130, 152, 157, 158, 161, 163, 164, 167, 169, 181, 182, 185, 187, 188, 191, 192, 194,
197, 210, 226, 231, 234, 237, 238, 280, 287, 307, 308, 313, 315, 316, 319, 322, 325; Neil Mersh 52;
Lis Parsons 10, 199, 200, 203, 204, 207, 241, 243, 247, 285; William Reavell 232, 268, 276.